A Kid's Guide to Drawing America™

How to Draw Georgia's Sights and Symbols

Jennifer Quasha

The Rosen Publishing Group's
PowerKids Press™
New York

To Sarah Unger

Published in 2002 by The Rosen Publishing Group, Inc.
29 East 21st Street, New York, NY 10010

First Edition

Book and Layout Design: Kim Sonsky

Project Editors: Jannell Khu, Jennifer Landau

Illustration Credits: Tom Forget

Photo Credits: p. 7 (Coca-Cola) © Corbis, (gold digger) © Bettmann/Corbis; p. 8 © (self-portrait) Georgia Museum of Art, University of Georgia; Extended loan from the University of Georgia Foundation, Gift of Mary and Lamar Dodd GMOA 75.12F, (sketch) Georgia Museum of Art, University of Georgia; Extended loan from the University of Georgia Foundation, Gift of Dr. Roy Ward GMOA 83.2; p. 9 © (painting) Georgia Museum of Art, University of Georgia; Extended loan from the University of Georgia Foundation, Gift of Mary and Lamar Dodd GMOA 77.6F; p. 12 © One Mile Up, Incorporated; p. 14 courtesy of the office of the Secretary of State, State of Georgia; p. 16 © Animals Animals; p. 18 © Bruce Burkhardt/CORBIS; p. 20 © Tim Zurowski/CORBIS; p. 22 © Ed Eckstein/CORBIS; p. 24 © William A. Bake/CORBIS; p. 26 © David Muench/CORBIS; p. 28 © Joseph Sohm; ChromoSohm Inc./CORBIS.

Quasha, Jennifer
    How to draw Georgia's sights and symbols / Jennifer Quasha.
       p. cm. — (A kid's guide to drawing America)
    Includes index.
    Summary: This book explains how to draw some of Georgia's sights and symbols, including the state seal, the Cherokee rose, and the bobwhite quail.
    ISBN 0-8239-6065-X
      1. Emblems, State—Georgia—Juvenile literature 2. Georgia in art—Juvenile literature
3. Drawing—Technique—Juvenile literature [1. Emblems, State—Georgia 2. Georgia 3. Drawing—Technique]
I. Title   II. Series
     2001
    743'.8'09758–dc21

CONTENTS

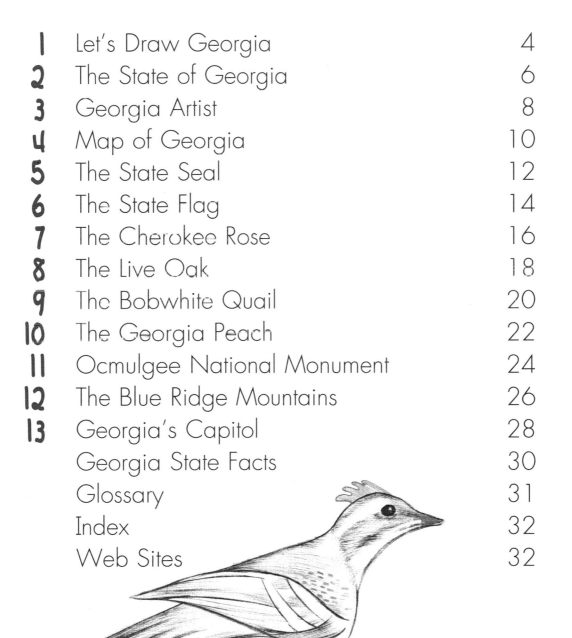

Let's Draw Georgia

A British man named James Oglethorpe founded the colony of Georgia in 1733 and named it after King George II of England. Native American Indians had been living on the land for centuries before Oglethorpe named it Georgia. Two groups of Native Americans who lived there were the Cherokee and Creek peoples. Many of the names of the rivers that flow through the state, such as the Ogeechee, Canoochee, Oconee, and Withlacoochee Rivers, come from Native American languages. Today Georgia is often called the Empire State of the South because it has been a leader in economic development among the southern United States. Georgia has played a key role in several American wars, including the Revolutionary War, the War of 1812, and the Civil War. Great heroes have been born in Georgia, including Dr. Martin Luther King Jr., who was born in Atlanta, the state's capital.

Georgia's natural beauty includes the peaks of the Appalachian Mountains, sandy beaches on the

Atlantic Coast, wild rivers, and fruit orchards. Georgia is a state full of beauty.

The step-by-step instructions and illustrations in this book will have you drawing Georgia's sights and symbols in no time! All the drawings begin with a simple shape. From there, you add other shapes. Each new step is shown in red. There are drawing terms to show you the shapes and words used throughout the book. The more you draw, the better you will get at it. Good luck and have fun!

You will need the following supplies to draw Georgia's sights and symbols:

- A sketch pad
- An eraser
- A number 2 pencil
- A pencil sharpener

These are some of the shapes and drawing terms you need to know to draw Georgia's sights and symbols:

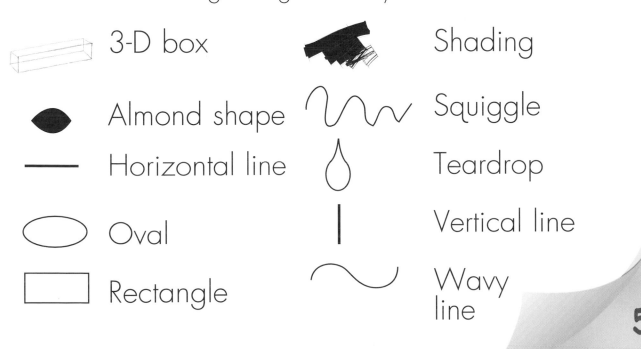

3-D box

Shading

Almond shape

Squiggle

Horizontal line

Teardrop

Oval

Vertical line

Rectangle

Wavy line

The State of Georgia

On January 2, 1788, Georgia became the fourth state to join a young nation, the United States of America. Today more than 7.5 million people live in the state. The largest city in Georgia is Atlanta, the state's capital. More than 400,000 people live there. In fact, about half of the people who live in Georgia live in or around the capital city. Atlanta is one of the fastest-growing cities in America today. Other large cities in the state include Savannah and Columbus. Georgia's land covers 58,977 square miles (152,750 sq km). It is the twenty-first largest state in area in the United States. California was the site of the famous gold rush of 1848, but America's first gold rush took place in Georgia. Gold was found in Dahlonega, a city in northern Georgia in 1828. Fifty-eight years later, John S. Pemberton of Columbus invented Coca-Cola, the world's first bottled soft drink. More than one million drinks of Coca-Cola are consumed each day. The company's headquarters is still in Atlanta.

Pictures of miners like the one shown at right suggested it was easy to make money during America's gold rush. Unlike gold mining, Coca-Cola is still earning money for the state of Georgia.

Georgia Artist

Lamar Dodd was an important figure in southern art during the twentieth century. He was born in 1909 in Fairburn, Georgia. Dodd studied art at the Georgia Institute of Technology and became an art teacher at the University of Georgia

In 1936, Lamar Dodd painted this self-portrait in oil on canvas.

in 1937. A year later, he was named the head of the university's art department. He taught at the university for more than 35 years. Today the school is known as the Lamar Dodd School of Art at the University of Georgia.

Dodd painted with great attention to detail and used color as a way to express different moods. He painted in many styles from

Dodd drew this sketch for a painting titled *View of Athens* in 1939. The sketch was drawn using ink and graphite on paper.

realism to abstract. In realism, painters show objects as they really are. Abstract artists use color, different brushstrokes, and textures to reveal feelings rather than realistic images. Throughout his career, Dodd painted Southern landscapes, city streets, portraits, flowers, and even sporting events. He also painted large, colorful images that celebrate NASA, the National Aeronautics and Space Administration. Dodd died in 1996, the day before his eighty-seventh birthday.

Lamar Dodd painted *From Our Campus* in 1941. He used oil on canvas to paint the work, which measures 19 ½" x 27 ½" (49.5 cm x 69.9 cm).

Map of Georgia

Map of the Continental United States

Georgia borders the five states of South Carolina, North Carolina, Tennessee, Alabama, and Florida. A small portion of Georgia's eastern coast borders the Atlantic Ocean. Georgia has many rivers and lakes, including the Chattahoochee and Savannah Rivers and the Richard B. Russell and West Point Lakes. The Okefenokee Swamp, a 660-square-mile (1,709-sq-km) natural wonder in southeastern Georgia, is a wildlife habitat. Georgia's plants and animals also thrive in its Chattahoochee and Oconee National Forests. Stone Mountain, a 1,686-foot (514-m) rock, and its park are popular landmarks for Atlantans who like to picnic on the weekends. Springer Mountain, part of the Blue Ridge Mountain range, provides great hiking trails.

10

1

First draw a large, rectangular box.

2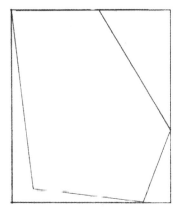

Next add the shape shown inside the box using four lines.

3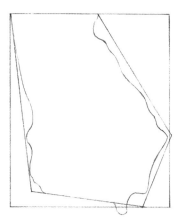

Begin to create the shape of the state's borders by drawing long, curved lines.

4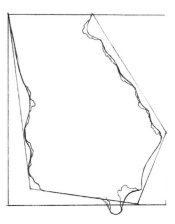

Add more detail to the outline using smaller, curved lines.

5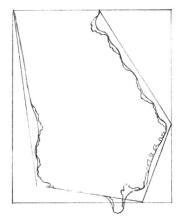

Continue defining the border in this step, again using small, curved lines.

6

To finish your map, erase any extra guidelines and add the key symbols shown for Atlanta (the state capital), the Blue Ridge Mountains, the Ocmulgee National Monument, and the Chickamauga and Chattanooga National Military Park.

Chickamauga and Chattanooga National Military Park

Blue Ridge Mountains

Atlanta

Ocmulgee National Monument

The State Seal

Georgia adopted its state seal in 1798. The seal shows three pillars holding up an arch. The word "Constitution" is written across the arch. A banner wrapped around the left pillar reads "Wisdom." The banner around the right pillar reads "Moderation." A third banner hanging above the center pillar reads "Justice." Together the three words become Georgia's state motto, Wisdom, Justice, Moderation. A soldier stands between the center and right pillars with his sword drawn. He represents the Georgia soldiers who helped to defend the U.S. Constitution. At the top of the seal, around the image, are the words "State of Georgia." Below the image is the date 1776, the year the Declaration of Independence was signed.

1

Begin by drawing a circle.

2

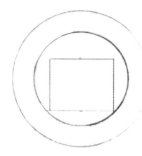

Next draw another circle within the first one. Draw a square box toward the lower part of the inner circle.

3

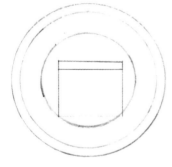

Draw a larger circle on the outside of the first one. Draw a straight horizontal line across the top of the box.

4

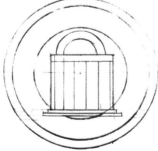

Draw two semicircles on top of the box. Draw six vertical lines in the box, and two horizontal lines with the bottom line longer, as shown.

5

Add another circle between the two outermost circles. Add six curved lines. Close the center curves with two vertical lines. Add three four-sided shapes as shown. Draw a thin rectangle at the top of the box.

6

Draw tiny lines in the ring's border. On the inside, add the shapes as shown to either side of the middle banner. Close the curved lines on the outside columns. Add more curved lines to make banners on the columns. Finish by drawing three squares at the bottom of each column.

7

To finish your seal, erase any extra guidelines. Use lines and boxes to make details on the roof and columns. Draw the man using three circles, a shape for his legs, and a line for his sword. Write the words of the motto.

The State Flag

On January 30, 2001, Georgia's state senate adopted a new state flag. This makes the seventh flag that the state of Georgia has adopted! At the bottom of the new flag is a banner displaying three earlier Georgia flags plus two American flags. Below the banner are the words "In God We Trust." In the center of the flag is Georgia's state seal. A circle of 13 stars shows that Georgia was one of the original 13 colonies. The new Georgia flag was adopted because the previous flag had two large bars in the form of a large *X*, which is a symbol of the Confederacy. Some people felt that the Confederate symbol brought back painful memories of the Civil War. Others felt that the Confederate symbol represented Southern pride.

1

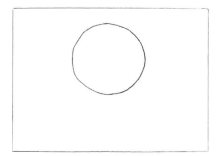

First draw a rectangle. Then draw a circle inside it as shown.

2

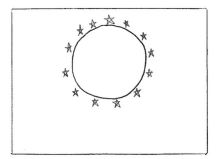

Draw 13 five-point stars around the circle.

3

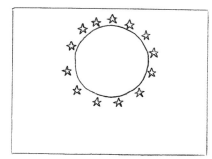

Erase the lines inside the stars.

4

Next draw a banner at the bottom of the rectangle as shown. Start with a curved rectangle and then draw the banner flaps.

5

Draw five rectangles inside the banner to represent the five flags. Add circles and stripes to the flags for the first, third, and fifth rectangles. Then draw a line, circle, and an X for the fourth flag. Draw an upside down U and an I for the second flag. Then write in "Georgia's History" on top.

6

Shade in the areas as shown.

7

In the middle circle, you can add the main shapes that you learned to draw in the Georgia state seal section (on page 13).

The Cherokee Rose

The Cherokee rose became Georgia's state flower on August 18, 1916. The Cherokee rose is not native to the United States. In fact, it came from China and was brought to America by English settlers in the 1700s. The flower, however, got its name from the Cherokees, Native Americans who planted it throughout the state. The Cherokee rose is a white flower about 3 inches (8 cm) in diameter. It has a large yellow center and dark green leaves, and it grows on very thorny stems. Groups of Cherokee roses are often used together to make garden hedges in Georgia. The Cherokee rose blooms in early spring, and often, again in the fall.

1

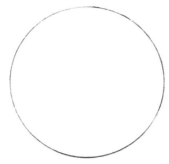

Draw a large circle.

2

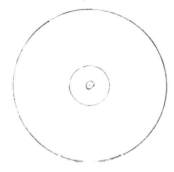

Draw two circles in the middle of the larger one. Make the one in the center very small.

3

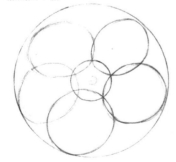

Draw five circles inside the larger circle. Have all of them overlap the circles on each side and the one in the middle.

4

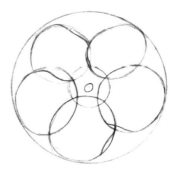

Draw curved lines at the edges of the circles to make flower petals.

5

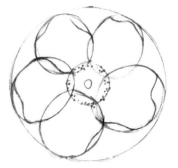

Continue using curved lines to finish the petals. Add many dark dots in the center circle.

6

Finish your Cherokee rose by shading the petals and the center. Draw more dark dots around the center. Erase any extra guidelines.

The Live Oak

In 1937, Georgia chose the live oak tree (*Quercus virginiana*) to become its state tree. Oaks are popular state trees because they grow for a long time. Like other kinds of oak trees, live oaks are big and strong, and they grow beautiful dark brown trunks and branches as they mature. Oaks also produce acorns. Many wild animals, such as deer, chipmunks, and squirrels, feed on acorns. Live oaks have oblong leaves that are about 2 to 5 inches (5–13 cm) long. The branches and leaves of a live oak tree spread out from the tree's trunk and offer shade during a warm Georgia summer.

1

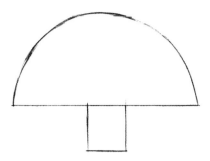

To draw a live oak tree, start by drawing a closed half-circle with a small rectangle beneath it.

2

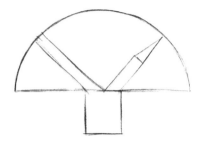

Next draw two thin, slanted rectangles and a small triangle at the end of one. These lines are the larger branches for the tree.

3

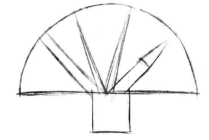

Now draw two long, pointed triangles. They will also be branches.

4

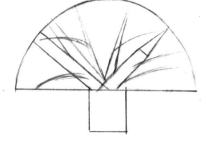

Draw another branch on the left side using two slanted lines. Then draw a series of curved lines that will be smaller branches.

5

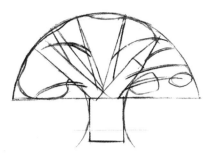

Start to create the shape of the tree by drawing curved lines and circles inside the half-circle. These will be clumps of leaves. Add long, curved lines on either side of the bottom rectangle to make a trunk.

6

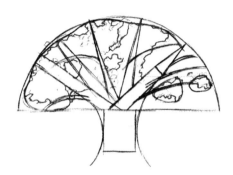

Next start to use smaller, curved lines to form the shape of the leaves on the branches.

7

Erase extra lines. To finish add shading and many smaller circles for the leaves. Make some of the circles darker for leaves that appear in the shade. (Leaves that are in sunlight appear lighter than those in the shade.)

19

The Bobwhite Quail

The brown thrasher is Georgia's official state bird. For their favorite game bird, however, Georgians chose the bobwhite quail in 1970. Like other game birds, quails are hunted for their meat. Bobwhites and other quail are so plentiful in the state, Georgia is known as the Quail Capital of the World. The bobwhite quail has a loud call, especially during the spring mating season. Bobwhite quails prefer to stay in small flocks while they walk or run across open fields. They feed on seeds, leaves, and roots. Bobwhite quails are about 10 inches (25 cm) long and have colorful, detailed markings. Both male and female bobwhites are covered with interesting combinations of brown, black, and white feathers.

1

Start by drawing a half circle that is closed by a slanted line.

2

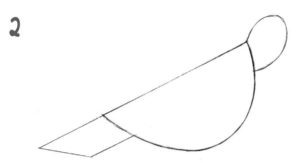

For the head, draw an oval to one side of the half-circle. Draw a tilted rectangle on the other side for the tail.

3

Add a wing by drawing a cone shape that overlaps with the half circle. Draw two curved lines that overlap the head. This is the bird's beak.

4

Draw curved lines for the bird's wing and tail. Add the lines as shown for the legs.

5

Add more curved lines to shape the wing and tail feathers. Add curved lines to make the feet, and more slanted lines for the legs.

6

Now draw a small circle for the bird's eye. Add more curved lines to create extra detail in the wing, tail, and beak. Draw small lines to create its toes. Use triangles to add the feathers on top as shown.

7

Finish your bird by adding shading and curved lines to give more detail to the feathers. Darken the eye.

The Georgia Peach

It is believed that the peach originated in China. European travelers visiting China carried this delicious fruit back to their countries. Spanish priests who settled in Georgia planted the first peach trees there around 1775. After the Civil War, farmers began to grow peaches for profit. Before long, peaches became an important cash crop for the state. Georgia is now the third largest peach-producing state. Today Georgia grows peaches on more than 22,000 acres (8,903 ha) of land. Georgia produces more than 130 million pounds (59 million kg) of peaches each year. The peach is so popular in Georgia, it appears in the names of many Atlanta streets.

1

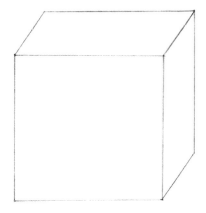

Start by drawing a three-dimensional box.

2

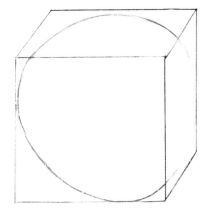

Draw a circle inside of the box.

3

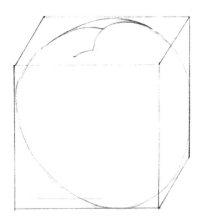

Next draw three curved lines at the top of the circle.

4

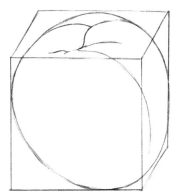

Draw three curved lines from the top of the circle, as shown here.

5

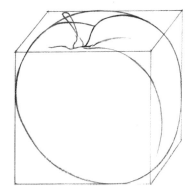

Make a stem by drawing a thin teardrop shape at the top of the peach.

6

Finally, add shading to your peach and erase the extra lines of the box.

Ocmulgee National Monument

The Ocmulgee National Monument is a 702-acre (284-ha) park. Ocmulgee means "boiling water" in Hitchiti, the language of the Creeks. The Creeks were one of the largest Native American tribes in early Georgia. Ocmulgee was the site of the first settlement of the Creek tribe. It is thought that the Creeks built their village around 1690, but there is evidence that humans have lived in the area for more than 10,000 years. Six temple mounds, one burial mound, and one ceremonial earth lodge still exist as proof that a large village was built in the area around A.D. 900. Today many people visit Ocmulgee National Monument to see the famous prehistoric mounds and earth lodges.

1

Start by drawing a rectangle with two slanted sides.

2

Draw a path by adding two curved lines that lead out of the bottom of the rectangle.

3

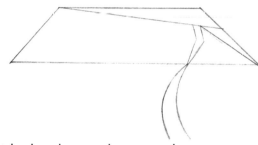

Inside the shape, draw two lines to create two triangles. Next draw two lines, as shown, that bend in the middle and meet in a point at the curved path.

4

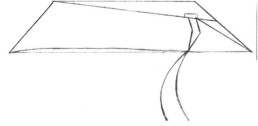

Next draw a small box at the top of the bent wedge shape. Draw a long, curved line along the bottom of the rectangle.

5

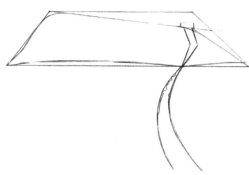

Add another curved line at the bottom of the rectangle. Use curved lines to add detail to the path and to round out the shape of the mound.

6

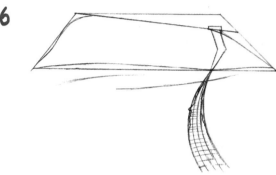

Make a pattern of straight and curved lines to create the stones in the path. Draw two long, curved lines beside the rectangle. These lines will show small hills.

7

To finish, add shading to the mound and the small, grassy hills in front of it. Draw short, straight lines along the side of the path to create blades of grass. Add some lines with shading to create the steps that lead to the top of the mound. Erase all extra lines.

The Blue Ridge Mountains

The Blue Ridge Mountains have a rich and interesting geological history. More than 200 million years ago, the Blue Ridge Mountains were created when the continents of North America, Europe, and Africa collided. The Blue Ridge Mountains are the eastern and southeastern ranges of the Appalachian Mountains. They extend from West Virginia into northern Georgia. Peaks in the Blue Ridge Mountain range can rise to 6,410 feet (1,954 m) above sea level. In addition to popular scenic trails that attract day hikers, there are many unmarked trails that are used and known mostly by hunters and fishermen. Native Americans called this area the Enchanted Land because of its beauty.

1

Start by drawing two open triangles, one smaller than the other.

2

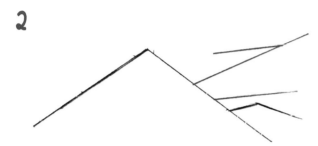

Add a few straight lines at a slant next to the large triangle.

3

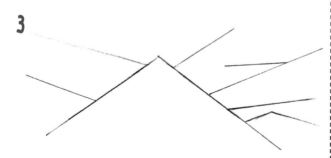

Next add several more slanted lines to the drawing.

4

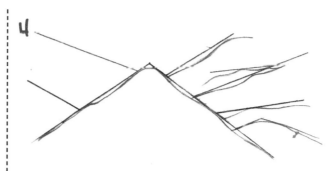

Start to create the shape of the mountains by drawing curved lines along the straight lines.

5

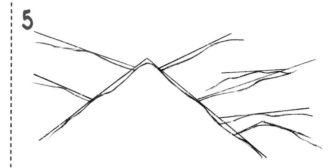

Continue drawing curved lines as in the previous step.

6

Add shading to the mountains and erase any extra lines.

27

Georgia's Capitol

The cornerstone of the Georgia state capitol building in Atlanta was laid on September 2, 1885, and construction was completed on July 4, 1889. The gold for the capitol's dome was mined in Dahlonega, Georgia, the site of Georgia's gold rush. Georgia and the state of Iowa have the two largest gold capitol domes in the country. There is a great mystery about the statue of a woman that stands on top of the dome holding a torch and a sword. No one knows who the woman is or what she represents, but many people have tried to solve the mystery. At night the torch in her hand is lit. The Georgia capitol building houses a museum filled with artifacts about the state's history.

1

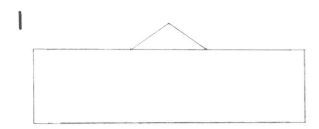

Start by drawing a large rectangle with a triangle on top.

2

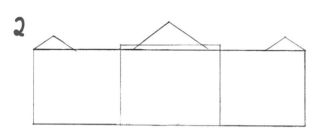

Next draw two smaller triangles on each side of the first triangle. Draw a smaller rectangle in the middle of the large one. This rectangle should be almost a square, and it should overlap the middle triangle a little bit.

3

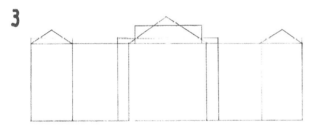

Draw two vertical rectangles on either end of the larger rectangle and one horizontal rectangle in the center, as shown. Draw two vertical lines from either end of the triangle in the middle.

4

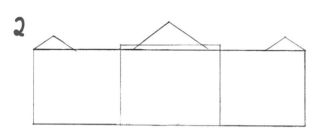

Draw a rectangle on top of the center rectangle. Draw a horizontal line across the middle of each lower rectangle.

5

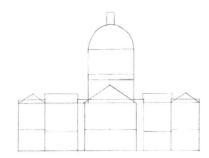

Draw a half circle on top. Add a rectangle to the half circle. Draw two parallel lines above the roof triangle, and two rectangles on either side.

6

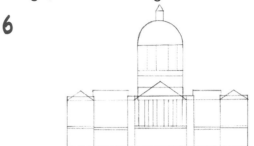

Draw 10 short, vertical lines in the middle of the center rectangle, and 4 more below the dome. Make a triangle at the top of the dome.

7

Draw in windows, then double the two roof lines. Draw 10 more vertical lines in the main rectangle. Double the lines below the dome.

8

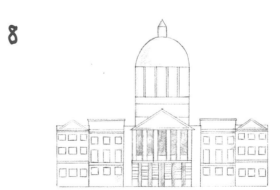

Add shading and draw horizontal lines across the bottom columns. Erase guidelines.

Georgia State Facts

Statehood	January 2, 1788, 4th state
Area	58,977 square miles (152,750 sq km)
Population	7,778,000
Capital	Atlanta, population, 401,900
Most Populated City	Atlanta
Industries	Textiles, clothing, transportation, tourism
Agriculture	Poultry, eggs, cotton, peanuts, peaches and other fruits, vegetables, cattle
Song	"Georgia on My Mind"
Butterfly	Tiger swallowtail
Fish	Largemouth bass
Fossil	Shark tooth
Gemstone	Quartz
Insect	Honeybee
Marine Mammal	Right whale
Mineral	Staurolite
Reptile	Gopher tortoise
Seashell	Knobbed whelk
Vegetable	Vidalia onion
Crop	Peanut
Dance	Square dance

Glossary

artifacts (AR-tih-fakts) Objects created and produced by humans.

ceremonial (sehr-ih-MOH-nee-ul) Having to do with a ceremony.

collided (kuh-LYD-ed) When objects have crashed into each other.

Confederacy (kun-FEH-duh-reh-see) The 11 southern states that declared themselves separate from the United States in 1860 and 1861.

Confederate (kun-FEH-duh-ret) Relating to the group of people who made up the Confederate States of America.

constitution (kahn-stih-TOO-shun) The basic rules by which a state or a country is governed.

diameter (dy-A-meh-tur) The measurement across the center of a round object.

evidence (EH-vih-dints) Facts that prove something.

geological (jee-uh-LAH-jih-kul) Relating to Earth's rocks and minerals.

habitat (HA-bih-tat) The surroundings where animals or plants live.

headquarters (HED-kwar-turz) The main location of a business or military department.

hedges (HEJ-iz) Bushes that often are used as boundaries.

mature (muh-TOOR) Grow older.

oblong (AH-blong) A long, oval shape.

originated (uh-RIH-jih-nayt-ed) To have come into being.

pillars (PIH-lurz) The strong columns that help to hold up a building.

prehistoric (pree-his-TOR-ik) The time before written history.

sea level (SEE LEH-vul) A way to measure how high or low something is on Earth's surface.

settlement (SEH-tul-ment) A small village or group of houses.

symbol (SIM-bul) An object or design that stands for something important.

Index

Web Sites

To learn more about Georgia, check out this Web site:
www.state.ga.us